ROBO-AUDITING

Using Artificial Intelligence to
Optimize Corporate Finance Processes

ROBO
AUDITING

PATRICK J.D. TAYLOR

with contributions by Manish Singh and Nathanael J. L'Heureux

LIONCREST
PUBLISHING

ROBO-AUDITING
Using Artificial Intelligence to Optimize Corporate Finance Processes

ISBN   978-1-5445-1144-3 *Paperback*
       978-1-5445-1143-6 *Ebook*

CONTENTS

INTRODUCTION

When you mention robots, most people think of *Star Wars* or those car-manufacturing assembly lines where giant, agile machines move heavy parts, make spot welds, or secure bolts on chassis.

Robo-auditing isn't quite as dramatic to watch, but the results can be just as astonishing. In the world of finance, robo-auditing combines automation and artificial intelligence to spot trends that humans often overlook and efficiently address any problems. It augments what humans do and enhances their effectiveness, speed, and efficiency. It's similar to the revolution we've seen in manufacturing robots, because the combination of automation and artificial intelligence in accounting is faster and more reliable than humans can ever be.

In finance, we've automated things for a long time. There are general ledgers, ERP systems, and spreadsheet programs like Excel. But robo-auditing allows you to do more than save time by automating these operations. It allows you to redesign business processes to increase efficiency and effectiveness. You don't just work faster; you work smarter.

Auto manufacturing is an example of how this should work. In the 1980s, American cars were not good quality, and the Japanese dominated the auto industry with less-expensive and higher-quality vehicles. At the time, the Japanese used a lot of robots in their manufacturing process, and Japanese carmakers were happy to let competitors tour their factories and see how they had automated so many steps.

American automakers came back and invested billions in robots to build their cars. The problem was that they automated the same work they had done before. They could make cars faster with fewer employees, but the vehicles were the same poor quality. They were not using these automation tools to redesign how they manufactured the cars. American automakers needed to refine and improve their work, not just automate an old approach that resulted in vehicles that broke down sooner than their Japanese counterparts.

Today, there is a lot more parity in the auto world,

because automakers have learned to use robots to build a better product.

The same thing is happening in finance. Although your company's accounting procedures are more straightforward than the quality challenges Chrysler, Ford, and GM faced back in the day, companies today find that artificial intelligence and automation help their financial people get their work done faster and more dependably than they could before these tools became available.

HELPING CFOS GET THE JOB DONE

The idea of using artificial intelligence to augment accounting and auditing procedures can sound intimidating if you equate AI with some of the more extreme ways it's employed today, such as in the development of self-driving cars. Fortunately, accounting doesn't offer as many challenging variables as designing a car to navigate the crowded highways around San Francisco.

But some CFOs are cautious for other reasons. The IT landscape is littered with shiny, new technologies that didn't deliver the ROI they promised, and this has made some chief financial officers reluctant to adopt the latest technological innovations. Most CFOs quickly get to this question: *Will my employees utilize this product and be willing to change their behaviors to take full advantage of it?*

Many products can address a company's real pains, but the challenge is adopting those products. CFOs want to know whether a solution can be integrated into their particular operation and help them achieve higher-value work.

I'm empathetic. When someone pitches me a product that promises to make my sales force more effective, it doesn't take me long to ask the same question: *Is this a good fit for our operation? Can I make that product work here?*

In my business of selling subscription-based Software as a Service (SaaS), we need customers to succeed. If *they* aren't successful, then *we* aren't successful. We depend on our customers renewing annually, and they won't renew if our product doesn't help them. This has taught us over the years to focus on the jobs that people are trying to get done. To go back to the auto industry analogy, we don't sell robots to help our customers weld their cars faster. We sell robots to help them build *better* cars faster, so they can be more successful. My robot is there to help you get done what you want and *need* to get done.

Artificial intelligence financial systems help CFOs do their jobs better, increasing their companies' profits while decreasing risk. As an example, we've seen across hundreds of robo-auditing implementations that companies can save an average of 5 percent just by analyzing travel expenses and educating employees to make smarter decisions. But that's only one place where artificial intelligence pays off.

IT'S MORE THAN CATCHING MISTAKES

When you explain how artificial intelligence improves corporate accounting, the first thing people think is that they can use a robot auditor to catch mistakes, for example, in expense reports. Maybe most of those mistakes are human errors, maybe some are fraud, and it's true that a robo-auditor will catch them.

But where the real money comes from is when CFOs, controllers, and CIOs use those audits to educate employees, so they don't make mistakes in the first place. Robo-auditing teaches employees to make smarter choices that stretch their travel budgets farther. Employees don't waste money as much as they used to, and that's what drives that 5 percent savings. It's less about, "Oh, I'm not reimbursing this particular item," and more about helping employees see the patterns in and implications of their behaviors, and driving financial impact by using analysis to improve company policy.

For example, say you have an account executive who travels to New York City. It's December—the most expensive time of the year to visit New York—and your executive spends $500 a night for her hotel room. That's what you'd expect to pay for a hotel around Christmas, and your robo-auditor doesn't flag that trip as an anomaly.

But say your executive travels to New York a few months later, when hotel rates are typically lower, and again pays $500 a night. Your robo-auditor—armed with data from thousands of expense reports not only from your company but from many other companies that also use the service—knows that is a bit extravagant for a trip to New York in March. It flags the expense and lets your executive know that the going rate for a quality hotel in Manhattan should be lower. The result is that in the future, the executive makes a better decision about where to stay and how much to spend. In this way, artificial intelligence steps in with the guidance an account executive needs to do her job more efficiently while saving her company money.

SO, WHY ARE CFOS CAUTIOUS?

Most CFOs are comfortable with automated financial processes. They've used general-ledger packages, and they know how to use them to get the most out of their businesses.

They can utilize artificial intelligence the same way. Fortunately, many business accounting practices are the same from one company and one industry to another, which means that CFOs who want to adopt robo-auditing don't need to build custom systems. They can buy packaged robo-auditors, just like they utilize packaged general-ledger systems, and then focus on smart ways to deploy them. They don't need to invent anything.

The applications of artificial intelligence and automation go far beyond examining travel expenses. For instance, CFOs can use robo-auditing to optimize their accounts payable and accounts receivable processes. Are you making erroneous payments to vendors? Are you paying them at the right time? You don't want to pay too early and tie up your working capital. But sometimes, paying early means you can earn a discount, so it may be worth doing. Your robo-auditor can guide your operations to pay at the perfect time.

How a corporation collects from customers influences both cash flow and customer satisfaction. A CFO's company may already do that well, but robo-auditing augments such expertise so that the company collects as expeditiously as possible while maintaining good customer relations. Robo-auditing protects your company's reputation by preventing flawed cases and quickly spotting malfeasance.

Robo-auditing can also smooth over the rough spots created when new employees come on board. New staff members can be prone to mistakes as they learn about your operations, but the robo-auditor notices when someone is making a mistake and helps new employees identify a better decision. The expertise built into the software means you don't have to worry about lost knowledge when you lose an experienced staff member. The robo-auditor helps you maintain consistent performance.

Robo-auditing is not a moonshot for your company. Someone else has already taken the moonshot and figured out how to do it. What's available now to CFOs is a packaged process that's practical and pragmatic. AI is improving, thanks to increased computing power that wasn't available ten years ago. Robo-auditing using AI and automation has moved beyond "Do I need to take this risk?" and is at the point where the risk is in *not* adopting it because your competitors already have (or soon will).

GETTING COMFORTABLE WITH AI SYSTEMS

This book will describe best practices for putting robo-auditing to work at your company. Again, CFOs don't need to invent anything; they just need to find the best way to apply robo-auditing to their operation and profit from it.

The best way for CFOs to get familiar with artificial intelligence is to start with the well-proven approaches that others have already automated successfully. Start with bite-sized chunks, employing robo-auditing on straightforward business processes like travel expenses or accounts payable. As you gain more experience, you can use it on more complex processes. This approach allows you to learn the system and identify the best ways to apply it in your operation.

Start with the common decisions and judgment calls that your people make. The payoff is higher when you automate processes that occur frequently rather than occasionally. You want to start where you can get a lot of repetitions quickly and get comfortable with the approach.

Accounts receivable are a good example. Since accounts receivable are handled the same way across all business units, many companies unite those functions and address them through a shared-services structure. A robot is a great way to make that centralized organization work more efficiently. You can buy prepackaged applications that have already been vetted by peer organizations who have developed best practices for applying the technology. As a CFO, you can leverage that expertise and focus your efforts on how to roll the system out successfully.

WHAT YOU'LL GAIN FROM THIS BOOK

Investors know that they often have to take risks to earn a high reward. That is not the case with robo-auditing. As this book will show, the risk of robo-auditing not working at your company is low, and the returns are very high.

I also want this book to be a practical guide for how CFOs can make robo-auditing systems work at their companies. I'll show you how you can walk, then run, with these capabilities. We've learned a lot about how to use the technology—that's what you buy our product for—but we've also learned a lot about the human and change-management aspects of adopting a capability like this. This book details the best practices that will help CFOs realize the system's potential.

HOW I GOT HERE

I got my undergraduate degree in mechanical engineering from the Georgia Institute of Technology in 1986. It was a traditional engineering degree, and one of the lasting things I learned had to do with closed-loop control systems.

That's the idea behind designing a system to monitor and control a process by measuring its output against your objectives and making adjustments to the inputs to keep the system on track. This process allows you to compare the actual result to the desired outcome in a way that enables you to reduce errors. If the system is disturbed, you can use the feedback to bring the output back to original levels. If you measure your output and compare it with what you wanted it to be, you can make adjustments to eliminate the discrepancies.

A traffic light is an example of this. One objective is to minimize unnecessary wait times. Nothing is more annoying than sitting at a red light when there is no cross traffic.

An open-loop-control traffic signal is set on a timer: it's green for two minutes, then briefly yellow, then red for two minutes. Thankfully, you don't see those much anymore, because most lights today are on a closed-loop-control system. They have sensors that tell them when a car pulls up. The signal will be set primarily on green for the busy road until a car pulls up on the less-busy street, and then the light changes. More sophisticated sensors can tell when cars line up on one avenue, or when there is a line of cars waiting to turn left. All these are examples of taking feedback from the environment and adapting the system to achieve the objective of keeping traffic moving.

Two years after graduating from Georgia Tech, I got accepted into the MBA program at Harvard Business School, where I took a course by James Cash called Management Information Systems. Cash taught us that the real computer revolution would come when we used computers to change *how* we worked as opposed to automating the work we were already doing. I wanted to be part of that revolution, so I embarked on a career in technology.

At the time, Oracle CEO Larry Ellison decided to hire more strategic sales people and ordered his managers to hire fifty newly minted MBAs with experience in the information-technology business. (I didn't qualify on the second count, but after weeks of persistent follow-up, they gave me a shot, anyway.) I worked with relational databases, which at the time were about doing analysis to make smarter decisions, and then went to work for Symantec. In 1996, I moved from Silicon Valley to Atlanta to work for a small company called Internet Security Systems.

Our software measured how well the security functions of a network of computers worked. We would know how a system should work, and what activity we should see, and compare that to what was happening. This process allowed you to spot any activity that wasn't supposed to happen and alert you to the presence of hackers that may have gotten into the system. We applied closed-loop controls to information security. I joined the company as employee Number Twelve and left about five years later when we were fourteen hundred people, and the company had gone public. IBM bought the company for $1.6 billion in 2006.

I co-founded Oversight Systems, Inc. in 2003 with the idea

of applying closed-loop control to the world of finance. Although companies lose a lot of money to hackers, they lose even more through internal fraud and waste. We were fortunate to hook up with Dan Kuokka, who has a PhD in Artificial Intelligence from Carnegie-Mellon, and develop what has become Oversight Insights On Demand, which currently provides solutions for Travel and Expense, Purchase Cards, and Procure-to-Pay, and will be expanding to additional business processes in the future.

At the most basic level, these systems find problematic transactions. But more importantly, they allow managers to zero in on the people who are causing the problems. There is usually a small number of actors who commit most of a company's errors, and when you identify those behaviors, you can set up process improvements to minimize the damage. Instead of chasing after and extinguishing a series of small fires, you can make process improvements and people improvements to keep those fires from starting in the first place.

Our clients include many Fortune 500 technology companies. These are companies that build their own artificial intelligence systems for product development and research, but they use our turnkey financial AI systems because this makes more sense from a time, effort, and effectiveness standpoint. We relentlessly work on problems in finance and accounting because those are the most essential things in the world to us. Our clients didn't invent their own financial AI systems, because we already had a tested and proven one. This allows them to put their researchers on more strategic projects. There was no reason for them to reinvent the wheel when it came to automating financial processes.

As we matured as a software-as-a-service business, we focused on how to make these tools work best for individual companies. We've deployed more robot auditors than anyone on the planet, and, as a result, we've learned a lot about how to best use AI in finance processes. Often in the technology field, you tell potential customers, "Hey, we've got this great set of capabilities that can do a million things; what would you like it to do?" But we've learned that the best approach is simply to tell people, "This is how you should do it." That's not meant to sound arrogant. It's just that we've developed the best practices already.

The purpose of this book is to share these best practices with you. On these pages, you'll see how to make robo-auditing, with its combination of automation and artificial intelligence, a success in your organization.

Are you ready to make that happen?

1

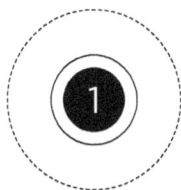

ARTIFICIAL INTELLIGENCE: CORPORATE FINANCE BENEFITS

Most large companies already have systems that automate basic tasks and have preventive controls in place to catch apparent problems. For the most part, this is black-and-white-oriented logic that generates strict rules for controlling very distinct outcomes.

But in the real world, not everything is so black and white. Some actions fall into gray areas and require exceptions to standard practices, and it's hard to address those activities with black-and-white rules. When you create preventive controls to attempt to deal with every possibility, you create a needlessly bureaucratic and suffocating system that interferes with productive work. You'll exert significant effort for ever-decreasing returns and end up with brittle systems. Plus, it's nearly impossible to cover every possible contingency. You need something better than the diminishing returns of increasingly restrictive black-and-white rules.

Diminishing Returns for Preventive Controls

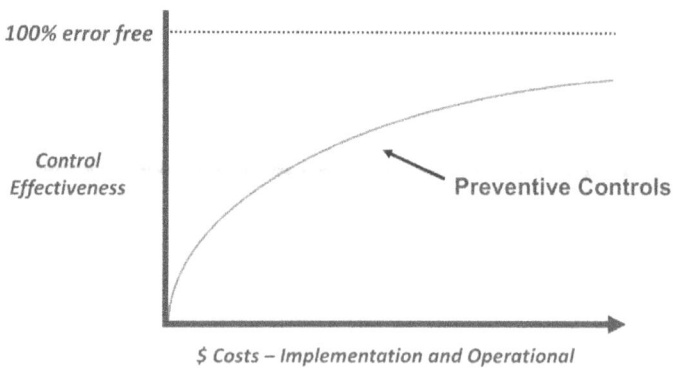

Robo-auditing replaces those suffocating rules. Robo-auditing brings ever-more-discerning analysis to those gray areas. You can still have your black-and-white rules, but they don't need to be overly constrictive; your artificial intelligence provides automated judgments that help you control the exceptions you often have to deal with in business.

What's more, every problem your robot spots is an opportunity to learn and refine the system. Consider the traffic-light analogy. You set up black-and-white rules so that when the sparse traffic from the west triggers a light change, it gets a forty-five-second green. But then your robot notices that on Tuesday afternoon at 1:15 when the Kiwanis Club lets out, the traffic from the west gets backed up. It refines the rules so that, from 1:14 to 1:19 on Tuesdays, westbound traffic gets a green light for ninety seconds, so the Kiwanians can get back to work after their meeting.

DISCERNING THE TRENDS

Using artificial intelligence, a CFO sees not only problems but the patterns in those problems. By observing the patterns, you get the information you need to figure out a process or policy change that makes things work better. It's a very Six-Sigma-oriented view of the world: you find the areas where you have a regular set of problems and figure out how to eliminate them from the system.

For example, we worked with a global chemical company that occasionally made erroneous payments to vendors. It overpaid some vendors, underpaid others, and paid some vendors twice for one job. The situation was further complicated when the company moved its accounts payable operation to Czechoslovakia to take advantage of cheaper labor. The company hired employees who knew even less about the company's operations than before, and managers worried that the risk of incorrect payments would increase.

The company had plenty of black-and-white rules in place to prevent these erroneous payments, but life's not perfect.

We analyzed six months of historical data. We wanted to identify the errors, but more importantly, we wanted to see what parts of their payment process allowed the errors to occur.

We found four thousand instances where they had made erroneous payments. That's only four thousand out of hundreds of thousands of payments, but it was a meaningful amount of money.

At that point, the company hired a recovery auditor to recover these erroneous payments and claw back the money from the vendors. The company would recover 80 percent of these incorrect payments—a significant chunk of change.

But the company quickly saw that a more significant long-term gain would come from a system that prevented those erroneous payments in the first place. The company could conserve its cash and not lose 20 percent of the funds to a recovery auditor. We deployed a robo-auditor to evaluate accounts payable transactions and prevent improper payments *before* they "cut the check."

The company enjoyed crazy ROI when it put the robot to work. Executives earned back the cost of our system in just six months. At the time, we sold our product as a perpetual license, meaning they bought our software and deployed it. If it had been a Software as a Service (SaaS) environment, like the one we have now, they would have recouped their investment in a month or two. What drove up the value proposition for them even more, however, was the fact that the robo-auditor identified opportunities to improve the process to prevent future mistakes. The savings just kept coming.

Another analogy to illustrate the value of artificial intelligence in corporate financial systems is the difference between X-rays and MRIs. X-rays are a tremendous diagnostic tool in medicine because they show what's going on with people's bones. But X-rays give a black-and-white result, and what you see is limited. MRIs, on the other hand, take it to a higher level and show you what's going on with your soft tissue—your muscles, tendons, and ligaments. With that broader set of information, you can figure out how to treat a problem and how to prevent that problem in the future.

ROBOTS VS. HUMAN AUDITORS

Even the best, most experienced human auditor has to take a back seat to a robo-auditor. Technology has a better memory than any human.

Most companies have a threshold for when an employee needs to produce a receipt for travel expenses. For many companies, anything under twenty-five dollars doesn't require a receipt. Can a human auditor remember how many under-twenty-five-dollar expenses a particular employee racked up over the last six months? Can a human remember that an unusually large percentage of the breakfasts and lunches and taxi rides this one employee has had over the previous six months was just barely under twenty-five dollars? No. But artificial intelligence can. A robot can spot that this employee submits twenty-four-dollar expenses at three times the rate of other account executives. A robot can quickly see that pattern and flag it.

Another advantage of robots: they don't suffer from positive confirmation bias. Confirmation bias results when anyone examines transaction after transaction and the vast majority are correct. When just about everything, time after time, is accurate, it's difficult for humans to condition their minds to find things that are not okay. When they're *expecting* everything to be okay, the tendency is to see the next thing as being okay.

A computer with sophisticated artificial-intelligence algorithms doesn't have the same burden. For most companies, only a small percentage of its transactions have problems, but flagging those problematic transactions is like searching for needles in a haystack. It costs more to manually locate the needles than you make from correcting the problems you find. But now, technology can look through all that hay and come back with a stack of sharp things for the human auditors to examine. The humans won't suffer from confirmation bias, because they have a lot less to look at, and everything in that pile of sharp things is at least interesting. And since many of those sharp things turn out to be needles, there is a much better return on your investment of time.

DETECTING PROBLEMS

Since it's impractical to develop controls to prevent every contingency, most financial systems rely on detective controls. When human auditors try to identify things that are not working, they typically use a manual sample-based approach and only do so every six months or once a year. Because 97 or 99 percent of the transactions are okay, odds are the sample won't have any errant transactions. And when most checks come back okay, there is a confirmation bias that works against human auditors who poke around for anomalies.

Robo-auditors, on the other hand, change that equation. With a robot, your detective controls are especially useful. The robot never gets tired and has no confirmation bias. It's fast and relentless.

Better detective controls give you better preventive controls. When you see a problem happening under certain conditions or circumstances, you can put something in place to avoid it in the future. It's always better to prevent a mistake than to correct it after it's occurred. But even if the percentage of errors is small, their detection and resolution can have an impact.

Robo-auditing, with its combination of automation and artificial intelligence, also gets smarter about spotting anomalies. Robo-auditors continually expand their knowledge base, and this makes them more efficient at spotlighting these abnormalities.

As you continue to use a robo-auditor, your financial processes get better. But there are always opportunities to improve. Your pile of needles may get smaller and smaller, but AI systems get smarter and more efficient in finding them. Just like quality in manufacturing, you can always improve.

If you're confident you're perfect, then we probably don't have anything to discuss. But business always changes: the transactions running through your system change, your employees change, and the business environment changes. It's not a static environment. You always have new challenges and thus opportunities to improve.

You may decide not to look for those opportunities. But your competitors certainly will.

REAL TIME VS. RIGHT TIME

Another interesting current concept is that you should identify problems in "real time." Although many people think "real time" is the be-all and end-all, it is often more effective to act at the "right time" when it comes to corporate finance.

For example, if you have a dramatic or sudden health problem—a stroke or a gunshot wound, for example—you need to get to the emergency room right away. To save your life, doctors must treat you immediately. But if you have a cold or a sore throat, you shouldn't go to the emergency room, because it's more efficient and cost-effective to see your family doctor. By the same token, if you have health problems related to obesity—and a lot of people in our country do—that problem is better addressed with counseling and lifestyle changes than a visit to the emergency room.

We have very few gunshot wounds in corporate finance. You might use artificial intelligence to immediately stop a fraudulent wire transfer if your robo-auditor spots it, but for most problems, the right time to attack them is not always in real time. You must be mindful of what your analysis shows and what actions you must take to correct the problems.

The robo-auditor allows you to observe patterns of wasteful spending. While you might flag the expense report from an account executive who lavishly overspent on a trip to New York, the more significant benefit is in using the robo-auditor to train people to make smarter decisions in the future. The robo-auditor can flag instances where that account executive didn't make an optimal spending decision and explain how the executive's travel budget would be affected if those costly mistakes continued over the course of a year. That's a "right-time" decision that gives you a better long-term result.

Most of your opportunities to improve will come from influencing future activities, not just from correcting a particular problematic transaction. You don't need to come down like a ton of bricks on the executive who booked a room in the wrong hotel. That hurts morale. But you *do* want to discourage her from booking there again, and you want to prevent other account executives from lodging there when they could have an equally good experience for less money elsewhere. Use your artificial intelligence to show people the net effect of their smaller decisions. Show executives that avoiding these hotels will stretch their travel budgets so they can afford to make more trips for the same money. More trips mean more revenue for the company and higher commissions for the executive. Everyone wins.

The "right time" depends on what you try to influence, control, or fix. If you use AI to drive an autonomous car, you want to instantaneously correct course to avoid that tree. But if you seek to prevent duplicate payments, you need to check things as frequently as you make payments—whether it's daily, weekly, or whatever. You don't want to change corporate policy concerning travel every five minutes, but it might make sense to re-examine it every quarter.

For any kind of process improvements, it's important to see patterns and not just individual events. To see patterns, you need to look at things over a longer period.

OTHER AREAS WHERE AI HELPS

Artificial intelligence provides significantly better oversight not only in the travel-and-expenses category but also in other business areas, including purchase cards; accounts payable; accounts receivable; contingent labor, credit validation, and payments; and accounting and currency hedging.

These are all areas where CFOs have a lot of instances to consider; AI sorts through all that hay to find the needles for you and the bigger picture issues behind those needles. We refer to this approach as the Three Ps:

- Problematic Transactions
- People's Behavior
- Process Improvements

The robo-auditor can find the problematic transactions, show you which actors need to have their behavior influenced, and help you drive meaningful process improvement.

Many corporations use manual detective controls. But human auditors are expensive, and the return on that investment might not be high enough—particularly when your human auditors miss needles because of their positive confirmation bias.

AI, on the other hand, can locate those needles and discern the trends that help CFOs drive improvements. AI spots enough of the needles to reveal the patterns. Now, the juice is worth the squeeze.

One of our clients, a Fortune 200 utility company, had a problem with accounts payable and used recovery auditors to claw back erroneous payments. The problem was that the utility lost the timely use of the money it had mistakenly paid and then lost the 20 percent it paid to recovery auditors.

When the utility employed robo-auditors, it discovered how many of those erroneous payments were made in the first place and improved the process. Now, before someone hits the wire transfer button, he or she runs the transaction through one of our systems. That process improvement has saved the utility $1.5 million in cash, plus the $300,000 to $400,000 that would have gone to recovery auditors. The robo-auditor, with its combination of automation and artificial intelligence, buttoned up the process so well that the recovery auditors eventually quit the account because there were no erroneous payments to reclaim.

Another client, a global beverage company, eliminated manual audits of its expense reports, reducing its T&E audit staff by 40 percent.

Wouldn't you like that to happen at your corporation? Read on to find out how.

2

ARTIFICIAL INTELLIGENCE 101

Most corporate financial systems focus on black-and-white math—the kind of calculations done in an Excel spreadsheet. It's meant to be very crisp, exacting, and discrete.

But much of the real world is gray. Corporate financial systems are digital and precise, but our world is still very much analog. We can put things in black-and-white buckets, but at times we need to interpret those numbers. Traditional transactional systems are not designed to handle that, but artificial intelligence is. As the name suggests, artificial intelligence replicates human logic. It mimics a human's ability to look at data and decide what it means. It makes a judgment call. It simulates human reasoning.

What's more, an AI-and-automation system can be taught to apply those decisions consistently and tirelessly. While human decision-making can be more nuanced than a computer program, a robo-auditor can apply its judgments all day long against mountains of detail. A human brain asked to repeatedly do the same thing would tire and grow numb. But a computer never gets bored or tired, and its mind never wanders. It is constant, dependable, and repeatable. Because of that, it's also highly scalable.

A general-ledger system has rule-based preventive controls that allow you to determine what you want and what you don't want to happen. A simple example of these preventive controls is when you have, say, a field that's only supposed to have numbers in it: the system won't let you type in any letters. Or, if someone is authorized to spend up to ten thousand dollars, they can't put ten thousand and one into the PO field.

It's impossible to write a preventive control rule for every contingency, however. If you try, you get a very bureaucratic system that restricts business activity, and with each new rule it becomes harder to maintain—the system becomes brittle. You end up trading off efficiency in an attempt to handle all of the potential risks.

Controls and Bureaucracy

Rigorous
Controls

Complete
Empowerment

Operational Risk   Operational Efficiency

Think back a few years to what it was like to buy a cell phone and sign up for cell phone service. The process was laborious and often took thirty minutes or more as the sales representative filled out all the requisite forms and asked you dozens of questions. All of this was necessary to ensure you got the plan you wanted and were billed correctly for the services you signed up for. The system was also designed to eliminate fraud.

Today, the process is much smoother and faster. The wireless carriers have automated their controls to where the process takes just a few moments. In fact, you can usually change your terms of service right from your phone if you want to. This kind of automation not only saves customers time, but it also makes it easier for the carriers to sign up new customers and cut wait times dramatically. Efficient customer interactions are good for business—and a good example of how automation can replace overly restrictive practices that only serve to slow down business and irritate customers.

Without a robo-auditor, detective controls require that

a person audit transactions to find problems in the gray areas. When your company has a high volume of transactions, this means the best you can do is sample audits. But even sample audits are expensive, and since preventive controls work the vast majority of the time, you also have the problem of positive confirmation bias even when your auditors are only doing sample audits.

But a robo-auditor does this quickly and accurately. Its mind never wanders. A robo-auditor allows you to institute superior detective controls, and superior detective controls allow your employees to work in a system that isn't overbearing and bureaucratic. That helps your business by increasing its flexibility. More relaxed preventive measures are sufficient when you're confident that outlier risks are monitored. For example, you can increase purchase-card limits and enjoy the greater rebates and other efficiencies that result. You have the best of both worlds.

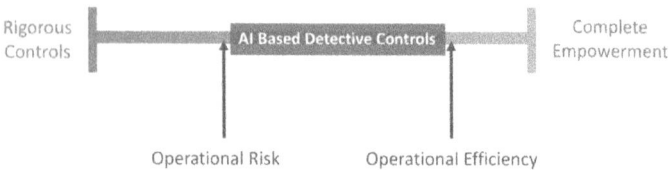

Rigorous Controls ——— **AI Based Detective Controls** ——— Complete Empowerment

Operational Risk   Operational Efficiency

AI JUDGMENT VS. HUMAN JUDGMENT

AI judgment calls are not as discerning as a human's. A human might know the person who conducted a particular transaction. A human may have overheard something around the water cooler and have some inside information that allows them to exercise better judgment. Your AI system may not be as plugged into the world or have as much subtle knowledge as a human auditor.

But, as we've mentioned, humans get tired. They look at so many proper transactions that they get confirmation bias and assume that even faulty transactions are acceptable. Humans can get overwhelmed with the details.

So, how do you keep human judgment in the decision-making process? You do that by allowing artificial intelligence to poke through the haystack, put together a small pile of sharp things, and let a person sort through *that*. You keep a human in the loop and let them use their superior knowledge and judgment to look through that small pile and find the needles. It's less tedious, and the transactions they analyze are all interesting for some reason, so the human can keep her mind tuned to find the needles. You get the best of both worlds: AI does all the heavy lifting, and a human mind analyzes the anomalies AI finds.

This system allows AI to learn from the human auditor. We'll talk more about this later in the book, but, for now, it's important to know that AI can watch how the human applies their judgment to the small pile of sharp things and learn from that. The next time you ask AI to search for needles, it comes back with a smaller pile with a higher percentage of actual needles.

If you allow the robo-auditor to "watch" what the human does, you create a feedback loop in which the software learns. AI looks at which problems the human fixes and which ones the human says are not real problems, and it acquires better judgment that it can use in its future work.

Artificial intelligence systems fall broadly into four categories. Real world systems often use a combination of techniques, but for simplicity's sake we'll explain them separately.

- Expert system
- Probabilistic or evidential reasoning
- Neural networks
- Machine learning

Here's a description of each of these four techniques.

EXPERT SYSTEM

This is the most basic form of AI. It codifies the rules a subject-matter expert uses to diagnose a problem. An expert, for example, might use a series of questions to narrow down his choices and reach a straightforward, yes-or-no answer. It's like a game of Twenty Questions. Initial queries are often broad, but gradually narrow as the expert whittles away the possibilities to reach a reliable answer.

The challenge with this type of system is that there are a lot of specific rules that take a long time to set up. Additionally, as things change, the work of maintaining and adjusting the rules over time is laborious. The benefit of these systems is that once the rules have been codified, they work tirelessly, accomplishing the same things that an expert can accomplish, but faster and without error.

PROBABILISTIC OR EVIDENTIAL REASONING

This is more dynamic than an expert system and is designed to find problems in gray areas. As humans, we look at many factors when making a decision, such as making a list of pros and cons. Detectives look for various clues when trying to solve a case, such as a partial fingerprint, a strand of fabric, phone records, witness accounts, and DNA evidence. Each of these clues has different levels of significance. DNA evidence is much more conclusive than a strand of fabric or a partial fingerprint. Evidential reasoning operates like a detective, looking for clues and applying weights to each hint to make some pieces of evidence more significant than others. As you look through the data and find more evidence, you become more confident that you've uncovered an issue. You can also consider negative evidence that makes you less confident.

Clues are known risk factors, both quantitative and qualitative, within the data. A quantitative clue is measured numerically, such as when one salesperson submits three times as many under-twenty-five-dollar expenses as everyone else. A qualitative clue requires some judgment, such as when you're asked to change a vendor's account to a Caribbean bank. That's not necessarily wrong, but it's a little suspicious.

The system looks for these types of risks, and the more risk factors it discovers, the higher your confidence is that the system has found something legitimately wrong. You can search for abnormal patterns: email addresses that are slightly different from a vendor's normal email conventions, addresses that are similar to but slightly different from previous ones, or invoice numbers that don't follow a company's regular pattern. These are things a tired human auditor might overlook, but an AI system will spot.

Let's take another look at the travel-and-expense rule that states employees don't need a receipt for any expense under twenty-five dollars. You look for employees who are cheating and making up expenses that don't require a receipt. A clue is when one employee has more expenses just under twenty-five dollars than all the others. When you find a unique pattern where every breakfast, lunch, and taxi ride is uncommonly close to twenty-five dollars, you have increased confidence that this person is up to something.

As the number of risk factors increases, so does the probability that you've found something. Once you have this probabilistic weight, you prioritize your actions and go after the riskiest things first. If you want to refine this further, you can multiply the probabilistic weight by the transaction amounts to come up with an estimation of what your return might be and use this figure to prioritize your actions. For example, you're only 75 percent confident about one transaction, but that transaction was for a million dollars. The "expected value" of seven hundred and fifty thousand dollars makes it a higher priority than a hundred-dollar transaction about which you're 90 percent confident.

You can also find problems with vendor invoices. For example, Facebook was recently defrauded of millions by a Romanian posing as a legitimate vendor. The imposter left several clues, including making a request to change the bank account number, which would have been flagged by an AI system using probabilistic reasoning. A robo-auditor, with its combination of automation and artificial intelligence, could have searched for an abnormal email or other addresses that didn't match up with that vendor's previous data, or it could have looked for a vendor invoice number that was out of order or had a different pattern than the vendor's normal invoices. All these clues could have been flagged by a robo-auditor but were very hard to spot without artificial intelligence.

The term "clues" suggests that you're always looking for wrongdoing, but you can also use these indicators to find new sales opportunities.

In marketing departments, this is called "lead scoring." For example, you see that a potential customer came to your website and gave you their name and email to download a white paper. You then send an email about a webinar you will host on the same topic, and the customer signs up and attends. That customer is assigned a heavier weight than someone who only visited your website and downloaded the white paper.

NEURAL NETWORKS

If you've ever gotten a call from your credit card company checking to see if recent transactions on your account were fraudulent, then you experienced the power of neural networks. Credit card companies are pioneers in using large data sets to discern patterns of unusual activity.

For example, if you use your card to buy gas, then go to the liquor store, and then go to an electronics store where you buy, say, eight big-screen televisions, you can expect to get a call from your credit card company. That's because, after years of tracking the patterns of fraudulent purchases on stolen credit cards, the company's AI system knows to flag that sequence of transactions. Thieves usually buy something small, then something bigger, and then go in for the kill with a big-ticket item. The neural networks employed by credit card companies recognize that kind of sequence and flag it.

Neural networks like this are set up to recognize patterns and mimic how the brain works. You feed a big set of training data into the network and identify the outcomes you are interested in, and the neural network develops its own logic for how to predict those outcomes based on the input data. The more practice data you feed it, the more experience it gets, and the more accurate its results.

You may go through several iterations of training a neural network on data sets. When the results from practice data are satisfactory, you can use the neural network on real-world data.

MACHINE LEARNING

Machine learning is when a machine is programmed to

learn in the same way humans learn and makes course corrections based on the data it collects.

For example, say you drive several different routes to work, and each one is different in some way. One way is shorter, but it includes a lot of traffic lights, making it a tedious drive. Another route is faster than the first route, but it also has heavy, unpredictable traffic. A third route is longer than the first two but faster because you can travel at higher speeds with fewer delays.

You drive these three routes several times, and then you take a step back and think about them. As humans, we do this all the time. We chose our first route because it was the shortest. Then we tried other routes, weighed each of their characteristics, and then settled on the longer route that takes less time and aggravation to navigate. We adjusted our original thinking that the shortest route was the best route.

The same pattern can work in a machine. In the first analysis, it looks for the anomalies that don't fit in the parameters we have set up. In accounting, for instance, the machine is looking for risks in financial transactions, based on an initial set of rules and known patterns of risk. At this first level, the machine might flag one thousand transactions that might have some risk.

Then the machine moves on to that second level. It

watches how humans treat each of those one thousand transactions. Some of these transactions are deemed safe while others are escalated as serious problems. The machine learns what are real problems and what aren't, and it automatically adjusts the criteria it uses to flag a potential problem.

In deep machine learning, there is even a third level where the machine uses the knowledge it has gained and refines the underlying rules on the first level. Lessons learned are fed back in and affect the first order of analysis.

Supervised learning is when a human is running data sets through the machine and teaching it what's right and what's wrong. Unsupervised learning doesn't require that complex pre-training data. Instead, the machine is looking at real-life data, suggesting outcomes, and learning as a human steps in and says yes or no to what the machine has suggested. The machine is constantly learning and refining its outcomes.

A robust robo-auditing system, like the one we offer at Oversight, is already very smart right out of the box. It gives good results immediately, because we know enough about the domains they work in—such as travel, expense, or accounts payable—to program in a strong set of first-level analytics. There are well-known best practices for these domains.

But even that well-trained, out-of-the-box system will keep improving and learning as it watches how you process the situations it surfaces. It's always learning and never gets tired. Read on to find out how this combination of artificial intelligence and automation can help you get more horsepower out of your company's engine.

3

ARTIFICIAL INTELLIGENCE & CORPORATE FINANCE PROCESSES

Corporate financial systems are well suited for using evidential reasoning as a starting point. It's a known world with known problems, so you have a strong starting point for designing the algorithms you need to produce evidence of problems that need to be addressed. You also know what the negative evidence—the information that makes you less confident that you've found a problem—looks like. You might already know all this information, but AI allows you to apply these judgments to mountains of transactions. AI goes through them faster and more economically and accurately than a human could.

Neural networks and machine learning can be more challenging, particularly if you don't have sufficiently large data sets to train them. With neural networks, the logic is embedded in the network itself, and it may return results that confuse you. "Why did it find this for me?" Because you may not fully understand the logic and the information the network returns, it can be difficult to remediate the issue. But these technologies play a key role, and we'll talk more about that later in the book.

A robo-auditor with automation and artificial intelligence makes sense for corporate finance because corporations have many years of financial data that are structured and consistent across industries—just what a robo-auditor needs to be effective. This world is more about optimizing than about inventing. We're not looking at billions of molecules to discover a new drug, and we're not building an autonomous car.

WILL I NEED TO DESIGN MY AI SYSTEM?

For most companies, if not all of them, it makes more sense to purchase a packaged AI auditing system than to design their own. Most companies already have packaged general ledger applications, so why not a packaged robo-auditing system? Problems caused by travel expenses and accounts payable are common enough across industries that packaged AI systems—designed by people who focus on finance—make sense.

Even if your company has data scientists—a luxury in a world where data scientists are in short supply—those scientists are more likely to be assigned to strategic projects, such as discovering a new drug. A CFO for that company will have a hard time getting a data scientist to break away from that work to design an AI auditing system, let alone maintain it and improve it in the future.

Those of us who build these packaged applications are entirely focused on AI auditing. That's all we think about. We learn from working directly with lots of companies, and we fold that knowledge back into our packaged systems. Prebuilt systems are easier to implement quickly, and our engineers are continually improving the system. Packaged systems get better with time.

These continual improvements come from looking across all of our clients all the time. We see a lot of scenarios— such as travel to a thousand cities in scores of countries around the world and purchases from thousands of vendors—that allow us to continually expand our knowledge of what's normal or unusual. Our data is far beyond what any individual company would have, and this makes our analysis more accurate and nuanced.

THE WISDOM OF CROWDS

Another interesting effect is what I call the wisdom-of-crowds issue. We might get a great idea from Chevron. We build it into our system, and then Google and GE can benefit from the improved analytics. The ideas from different customers are fed into the system to improve the analytics and the workflow. The system gets better because more people use it and more people give feedback that is folded into the application.

Most companies lack the resources and time to do that themselves. It's a lot easier and more economical for us to collect all of this data, because we have the resources and time to go through it. Here's an analogy: In the early days of the automobile, all cars were custom built from exact designs, and only rich people could own them. Then, Henry Ford came up with standardized designs that allowed a good car to be built cheaper. After that, you didn't need to be rich to own a car. Another example is customer management systems. Twenty or thirty years ago, you would have built one of those from scratch. It's rare for someone to do that today. Companies still build custom applications for processes that are unique to their business, but most companies buy packaged applications where they can.

The key question for corporations considering packaged AI auditing is: can the system be readily and easily adapted to meet your specific needs? The answer is often yes. Most accounting practices are similar from one company to the next and from one industry to the next. This is why packaged AI makes sense for more corporations and large companies.

In rare instances, a CFO might be reluctant to share data that might reveal a trade secret. For instance, if Chevron learns a smart way to find oil reserves, it won't share that information with Exxon. But when it comes to stopping fraud, T&E waste, or information security breaches, most companies are willing to share, even if it's with a competitor. In essence, it's similar to fire prevention. Even though it would probably benefit me if my biggest competitor suffered a fire, most people would take part in efforts to prevent a fire at a competitor's facility.

PUTTING AUTOMATION TO WORK FOR YOU

A robo-auditing system working with these rich data sets helps companies set up accurate and reasonable safeguards that would be laborious for their teams to create and expensive to maintain.

For example, you can get in trouble for taking a government official out for a string of extravagant meals. So, your company has to ensure its employees entertain government officials in a way that is normal and customary for the locale. But what constitutes a normal expense in these circumstances? What's normal in New York City might be extravagant in Sioux Falls, South Dakota. For international travel, you must take into account exchange rates and inflation, which is higher in some countries. These factors will have an impact on what is considered a reasonable amount to spend on dinner.

Theoretically, you could manually code specific rules for every major city on the planet. But that would take a lot of effort, and it would be expensive to update the rules as factors changed.

However, with a rich data set, you can put the computer to work for you and use machine learning techniques to establish a reasonable amount for a meal in any given country or city. The task is faster, doesn't require nearly as much coding, and the information stays current because the computer keeps learning as it sees more and more expenses. It recognizes trends in various global locations. The allowed reasonable amount for meals will change as the algorithms learn on an ongoing basis.

This process applies to hotel expenses as well, which vary from city to city and country to country and from one time of year to the next. For example, it's expensive to reserve a hotel in New York in December or July, but less so in February. Phoenix will be expensive in the winter but cheaper in the summer. Computers are more efficient for learning and identifying reasonable hotel expenditures. The more data you collect, the better it gets. This is the network effect kicking in. Scale matters.

You also want to be careful about how you learn from the data. Some companies are more strident about managing expenses than others. Some companies allow higher travel expenses when a manager approves it. Other companies will take the attitude that "Thou shalt always use one of our official hotels where we receive a negotiated rate." There is a lack of a fixed pattern between those two companies' approaches, and it takes artificial intelligence to figure out what's reasonable and which companies have more variability. AI can calibrate each company's contribution to the database by taking into account the company's variability.

HOW AI FOSTERS FLEXIBILITY

A robo-auditor, with its automation and artificial intelligence, allows CFOs to give their people more flexibility. A company can institute less restrictive controls because its detective monitoring will find problems. The added flexibility increases productivity and efficiency.

This is important because, in recent years, regulations have forced most companies to implement increasingly strict preventive controls to reduce fraud, such as when a person creates a fictitious vendor, inputs an invoice for goods never received from that vendor, and then approves payment to that vendor. This is one way an employee can steal from their company.

To stop this, preventive controls were put in place (particularly emphasized under the Sarbanes-Oxley Act of 2002), ensuring that the person approving an invoice is not the same person who created the vendor. It's called segregation of duty. Neither person can do both steps, so no one person can steal from the company.

Segregation of Duty as a Fraud Control

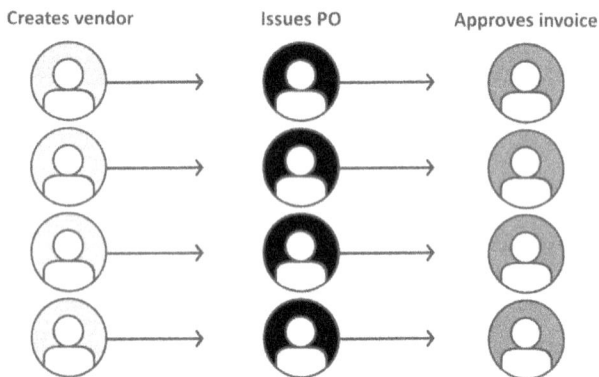

Creates vendor   Issues PO   Approves invoice

Before companies had a robot auditor, they either had to implement restrictive preventive controls, or they had to double-check every transaction, which is time-consuming and expensive.

But now companies can have a robot auditor check every transaction and make sure that an employee doesn't approve an invoice for a vendor he created. On the rare occasion when, in an emergency, an employee creates a new vendor and approves a payment to that vendor, the robo-auditor will flag it for a third party to inspect to ensure it was not a case of malfeasance. This quick and manageable approach greatly reduces the risk of fraud while fostering a more flexible work environment.

Flexible Work Environment with AI Fraud Control

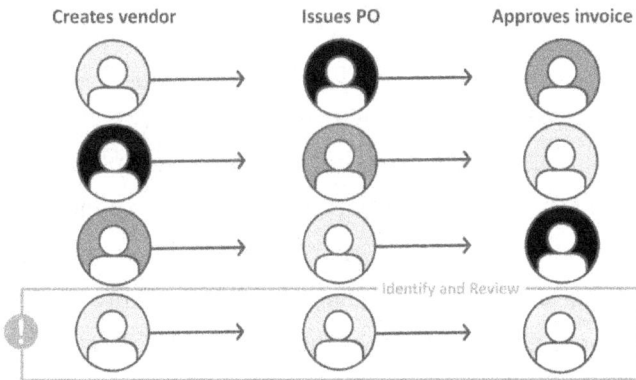

| Creates vendor | Issues PO | Approves invoice |

THE '60S MUSCLE CAR

Here's an example of how a next generation of detective controls improved efficiency. In the '60s we had the muscle cars, the GTOs for instance, and they all had mega horsepower and poor gas mileage. In the late '60s and '70s, the power of an engine—measured in horsepower—was largely related to the size of the engine. The very best performing cars generated close to one horsepower for each cubic inch of engine. Then, in the early 1970s, EPA regulations kicked in and made these gas-guzzling engines obsolete. But today, despite even more restrictive regulations, many new cars produce more total horsepower than the old muscle cars, with smaller engines. How did this happen?

Car manufacturers are using smarter, automated controls. Here's an example:

One method of improving the performance of a car is to change the point at which the spark plug ignites the gas in the system. The piston compresses the gas and air, the sparkplug lights, the gas burns (it doesn't explode as you might think), and that burning creates an expansion that drives the piston that turns the engine. When the engine begins to spin faster, you need to light that fire earlier to provide enough time for the gas to burn. That's called advancing the spark. During the Model T era, drivers advanced the spark with a lever on the steering column to optimize engine performance.

- Piston goes up
- Compresses the gas and air

- Sparkplug ignites the gas
- Et Voila – produces power

However, under some conditions, such as driving uphill with a heavy load on a hot day, the heat and pressure in the cylinder can ignite the gas, independent of the spark plug. This creates multiple flame fronts inside the combustion chamber. As the two fires burn, the pressure waves from each fire collide and create what's called spark knock. Instead of a single flame expanding smoothly to drive the piston, multiple flames create small shock waves that produce a pinging or knocking noise. Spark knock can cause all kinds of damage, from cracked pistons and rings to blown-out head gaskets. During the Model T era, drivers listened for the spark knock and wouldn't advance the spark as much when they heard it. (Driving a Model T well required a fair amount of skill.)

"Spark Knock" – Harms Engines

- **Heavy Load**
  - Uphill
  - Car full of passengers

- **Hot Day**

Automakers eventually developed systems that automatically advanced the spark the faster the engine operated. It worked well, but to accommodate for those hot days when you drove uphill with a heavy load, they limited how far the automated system could advance the spark—a preventive control. Consequently, you didn't get spark knock on those hot days when you hauled a load uphill, but you also couldn't take advantage of all the other times when it made sense to advance the spark plug a little more. You couldn't achieve better performance, because you needed to prevent that one bad thing from happening during that rare uphill climb in the summer heat.

Now in the computer age, cars are built with advanced monitoring devices. Your car advances the spark as much as possible but automatically backs off when it detects spark knock. So, because your car can detect and prevent this problem from happening in the rare cases it occurs, you can now take advantage of all the other times when it pays to be more aggressive. Modern cars rarely experience spark knock, because they monitor to avoid it. Whenever they can, modern cars take advantage of the more aggressive timing of the spark, giving you better performance. As a result, today dozens of cars produce higher horsepower than was available at the peak of the muscle car days.

In this sense, the robo-auditor is like the monitoring device in your car's engine. A robo-auditor gives you great detective controls (it has an ear for spark knock) and allows you to be less restrictive with preventive controls designed to prevent a rare problem (the spark knock that only occurs on those hot, uphill hauls). Before adding artificial intelligence to your accounting system, you may have had preventive controls designed to save you during that 1 percent of the time when you were metaphorically struggling uphill. But those preventive controls limited you the remaining 99 percent of the time when it's better to advance the spark. The superior detective controls in the robo-auditors throw off those limits and help you move ahead quickly and efficiently, confident you'll avoid any future spark knock risks.

DECISION MAKING: GETTING STARTED WITH THE WORKBENCH

The key to making robo-auditing successful at your company is not just the analytics but what actions you take based on that analysis. You want to focus on, "What can I do with this? What decisions am I going to make? How can I improve a company process?" The analytics are astounding and make you wonder, "How did it do that? Isn't machine learning amazing?" But the rubber meets the road when you decide what to do with that analysis. What do you do with the answers you've found?

The key is to focus on how to put those answers to work in your organization. The idea isn't to just spew out reports to people. You must consider how people will use these analyses to improve your processes. You want to improve an outcome or correct a process flaw. And this is where the robot side—the automation side—comes into play. How can you use automation to support those new processes and make them as efficient as possible? Done right, robo-auditing makes you smarter and faster.

The whole context of auditing is to check up on what's going on and identify and correct any issues. The gold star of auditing is to point out ways to improve the process.

NAVIGATING GOVERNMENT REGULATIONS

Here's a good example of how a global pharmaceutical firm used a robo-auditor to identify problems and took steps to prevent them.

The pharmaceutical industry is governed by numerous federal regulations regarding how money is spent when entertaining healthcare professionals. Pharmaceutical companies are vigilant about ensuring their employees follow policies on expense reports. There is little tolerance for error.

This particular pharmaceutical company had a staff of about twenty people tracking these problems, using spreadsheets and business intelligence tools. However, policy violations continued. The company didn't catch everything, nor was it changing future employee behavior. Again, the idea is to find problems and determine how to fix them in the future.

Often when we think about fixing future problems, we think about redesigning a process. However, in this case, the problems resulted from the decisions employees made while traveling and entertaining clients. So, the goal becomes educating employees to make more appropriate decisions.

This company faced not only the typical travel and expense issues—such as ensuring employees stayed in approved hotels—but also this additional layer about complying with federal rules on how much they spent entertaining doctors. It gets a little tricky. You might know how much you can spend taking the doctor out to lunch, but how much can you spend to cater a lunch for the doctor's office, and how much of that expense has to be applied to federal limits on what you can spend on that particular doctor?

So, the pharmaceutical firm implemented both the artificial intelligence, which helped them spot the problems, and an automated case management system to help them deal with the findings.

The result was that they were able to communicate with

employees and point out specific patterns of problems with their expense habits. They could also explain why those were problems. They educated their employees and put them on notice that someone pays attention.

Consequently, they reduced their compliance team by 80 percent while increasing compliance by 90 percent. That's a huge reduction in risk to the company. This prevents legal problems with government regulatory agencies regarding how you entertain health care professionals.

AI enabled the company to develop a systematic way to find problems and influence employees' behavior. That is what drives real impact. As a manager, you go from being a fire chief putting out fires to a fire marshal who prevents fires. The company saved money by reducing its compliance staff from twenty to five full-time equivalents and reduced its risk of fines or sanctions from the federal government.

For an account executive for the pharmaceuticals company, this keeps you out of trouble and saves your job. You're less likely to make mistakes, because your company has been very clear about what's okay and what's not.

PREVENTING DUPLICATE PAYMENTS

Most companies will have preventive controls in place to

prevent duplicate or improper payments. For example, when you have a purchase order for a specific vendor, that purchase order must be matched to a receipt for goods. That receipt, in turn, is matched to an invoice. If all those things match up, the payment can be made. If a second duplicate invoice arrives, you know that it has already been paid, because of the purchase order that was issued. That's how the world *should* work all the time, but there is no perfect world. Mistakes happen.

Say someone in your company issues a purchase order for a large supply of goods. Sometimes, those large orders arrive in different shipments, with a different invoice for each shipment that comes in. To complicate matters further, some vendors send invoices to everyone they know in the company. With multiple invoices going to different sources, it's possible for multiple copies of the same invoice to be mapped to the one large purchase order. One time that invoice gets entered as "1234", and another person enters it as "1234." and another as "001234". Now, your ERP system has a control that says that for any vendor, every invoice number has to be unique, as a way to prevent you from paying the same invoice twice. But while to a human it's obvious those are same number, to a computer 1234, 1234., and 001234 are different numbers.

The majority of the time, things work out okay and these types of duplications are spotted and corrected. But in some cases, they aren't. When a company has to manually look for problems like these, they are too hard to find, and the company figures, "This is a small percentage of our problems. We can live with it." Or they could pay a recovery auditor to comb through last year's payments. The auditors find mistakes, recover the extra payments from vendors, and take a share of what they recover.

But now, with sophisticated artificial intelligence, you can find those things yourself. With automation, you can even find them before you ever make the erroneous payments, so the money never leaves your company. You nip the problem in the bud. The AI system tells them, "We already paid invoice #001234, so we should not pay invoice #1234 because too many things look similar."

Sophisticated technology picks up on things that are different or unusual. At a flooring company we work with, someone ordering supplies clicked on 'boxcars' instead of 'boxes,' which meant they ordered a whole lot more than they wanted. But the system flagged it as unusual, and someone saw it and said, "Wait, wait, wait. We don't need to buy a boxcar of this stuff."

If companies aren't careful, they can end up with so much bureaucracy that it's hard for people to get the work done. With preventive controls, you get diminishing returns. You can induce so much overhead that you spend more time preventing problems than the problems would have cost in the first place. You must balance the cost of prevention with the cost of the problems you're trying to prevent.

A good AI system can create advanced detective controls that shift that cost balance in your favor. Robo-auditing makes finding and preventing those problems much more affordable. Companies don't have to accept the losses from duplicate payments; they can now easily identify and rectify those problems. They can even back off on some preventive controls. Like drivers enjoying spark-advance technology, managers and executives can be more aggressive because they know AI will catch the rare bad situations. That allows them to operate more efficiently and effectively.

FINDING INFLATED EXPENSE REPORTS

One of the easy ways to pad an expense report is through what is broadly termed out-of-pocket expense.

Let's say that you pay for your hotel with a corporate credit card. The company sees those bills and can verify how much you spent. But you pay for a taxi out of your pocket. You can be reimbursed for that. Or you can log mileage when you drive, and you will receive that mileage reimbursement. These are common places where people pad their expense reports and pick up some extra money. It's tricky, because there is typically a threshold of $25, or as much as $50 or $75, under which you don't need to produce a receipt, and that's not to mention mileage. It's easy to make something up. Even though there are specialized apps for phones that track expenses and miles traveled for business and will submit it on an expense report, most people don't have them.

With AI, you can begin to identify patterns of abuse over time. An employee's mileage may consistently seem higher than it should for the number of sales calls made or for the state the employee is traveling in. You will drive more miles to make sales calls in Wyoming than you will in Rhode Island. Artificial intelligence understands those factors and determines your employee's mileage, taxi rides, or meals don't look right compared to others in similar positions.

This information gives you, as the employee's manager, an opportunity to follow up with the employee. If the employee's behavior is egregious enough, you can initiate an HR action. But more commonly, you will try to educate the employee and let them know what you see through the robo-auditor. If you're purposeful in your follow-up with people and you have a way of tracking, you can then say, "All right, we warned you about this two months ago. We still see the inappropriate behavior." This way, you'll start to influence their future behavior. But you must be organized and purposeful about how you take action.

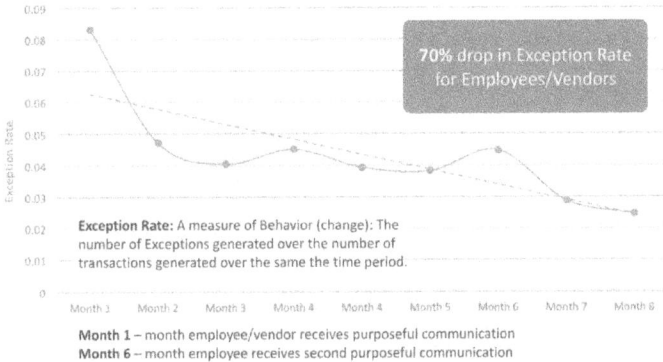

70% drop in Exception Rate for Employees/Vendors

Exception Rate: A measure of Behavior (change): The number of Exceptions generated over the number of transactions generated over the same the time period.

Month 1   Month 2   Month 3   Month 4   Month 4   Month 5   Month 6   Month 7   Month 8

Month 1 – month employee/vendor receives purposeful communication
Month 6 – month employee receives second purposeful communication

The first warning will usually correct the behavior. If it doesn't, the second one probably will—particularly if the employee knows you remember the first warning. If you have an organized, automated way of handling all this analysis, you can achieve better results and improve processes in the future. You can be more efficient in your follow-up and in your action on the results.

What you will look for in a robot auditor is the ability to inspect things, as well as the ability to resolve issues in an impactful way. That is not only efficient, but will have a long-term impact.

An international beverage company used this technology to reach an important decision. After flagging employees logging extensive mileage, they realized it would be more cost effective to give some employees company cars.

Another company had a policy that it wouldn't pay for employees to buy in-room movies in their hotels. But when they used AI to analyze expenses, it found that those who bought movies in their hotel rooms spent significantly less on dinners. The company changed their travel policy and now reimburses employees for in-room movies.

INSPECTION AND RESOLUTION

It's invaluable when technology not only finds these patterns but also records and learns how you respond. These are the two critical processes of robot auditing systems—the inspection and the resolution.

The inspection involves running the analytics and finding "exceptions" or potential problems that are unusual or don't follow the expected pattern. The resolution is what human managers do to address those problems. The data about those resolutions is fed back into the system, which allows managers to teach the AI system what's important. This feedback loop enables the system to get smarter.

When an AI system identifies an issue, it should also deliver supporting data so the manager has the context needed to resolve the issue. For example, the system might alert the manager to the fact that this employee has been involved in flagged transactions before. The information is all delivered to managers, so they don't have to spend time searching for it.

Here's an example of how inspection and resolution can work hand in hand. Say an employee submits an expense report for the purchase of digital artwork. Your company rejects the expense because it's not the type of thing an employee would normally purchase. But it turns out the employee works for the marketing department, which is putting together a new ad campaign that requires a special type of vector graphics. Suddenly, the expense makes sense. The marketing department has an ongoing need for graphics for its ad campaigns, so the manager indicates it is a legitimate purchase. Your AI system sees that and learns: digital artwork is okay for marketing.

In this case and others, it would be difficult to have blanket preventive controls in place, because the criteria for each department are so different. It gets too tedious to try to code all that in. But when the system can learn what to find and what to disregard in the future, the company can achieve increasingly efficient processes.

Buying cases of beer isn't okay for most employees, but it is for those in the catering group who supply items for customer visits. So if the robot auditor spots someone buying cases of microbrews and flags it as an anomaly, you can go into the system and note that employees in the event-planning department are approved for purchases like that. The machine learns not to flag beer purchases from that department in the future.

Machine learning can be accomplished through purposeful learning or by observational, patterns-based learning. You can provide a mechanism where the humans approve expenditures from particular departments. The machine learns to recognize those situations as less important.

AI can learn over time to be more precise. The first time you say that it's okay for the events people to buy alcohol, typically, is not enough for AI to learn. You can provide the instruction yourself—advanced systems make it easy for managers to teach the system—or you can allow it to learn on its own. The latter takes more time and repetition because machine learning requires a lot of data sets and patterns for the machine to learn effectively.

GETTING STARTED WITH THE ROBOT AUDITOR

As a CFO, you may have lots of great ideas for using the robo-auditor. However, the key is to start with something very tangible with a solid return. Seize on something readily achievable. Build some momentum and try to get some tangible results in the first month or two.

Robo-auditing can address a wide range of issues, but starting out, it's best to focus on one or two areas where the analytics yield a high degree of accuracy and you can get a good payback. You want users to get comfortable with the process and help them see that they had an impact before taking on more advanced and challenging tasks that might take longer to roll out and show results.

Working with artificial intelligence is a new competency for your company. You want to get used to using it, see what it's like, enjoy early success, and build trust in it. Start in a very purposeful way in a very discrete area. As your team gets comfortable and more competent in working with the robo-auditor, you can expand the scope of what the robot does.

AN INTRODUCTORY INITIATIVE

A great place to start using a robo-auditor is in travel expense reports. Many companies worry about those. Look for hardcore problems, such as people entering duplicate expenses. That's a pretty black-and-white problem. Mistakes are often innocent, but sometimes people are gaming the system. That gives you a start on using the new system, and it gives you something you can act on and get a return from right away. Down the road, you may also look for patterns of inefficiency in choices of meals and hotels when employees travel, but that issue might not be something you'd want to address in the first month. That and other problems are harder to wrestle to the ground and require changing the behavior of employees before you start to see returns.

The real critical factor is engaging your teams with the

robot. You don't want to overwhelm them by taking on too much out of the gate. Get them started, get them successful, and then you can iterate, improve, and build on what they learn. Most of the time your accounting department won't immediately abandon what it was doing in the past, such as sample-based audits, so, often, it will run parallel processes until it is comfortable with the robot and confident enough to stop some of the things they were doing in the past.

BIGGEST CHALLENGE IN IMPLEMENTING AI

Many AI systems produce stunning reports and dashboards. That part can be magic and automated, but analytics are just the beginning of the process. You need to focus on what you want to achieve with the insights produced by those analytics. What job are you trying to accomplish? Your goal might be to minimize the risk in travel and entertainment spending, or minimize the risk and optimize your use of cash in accounts payable. Whatever your goal, analytics play a role, but they're not the end result.

Your system needs to incorporate both the inspection side and the resolution. While the inspection and analytics are automated, the resolution is not. This is why you need an interface that incorporates both inspection and resolution. We happen to call that a workbench and will use that name as shorthand, but whatever the name, you want capabilities that allow you to automate resolution.

Think of this process as a case management system. Say your robo-auditor surfaces an issue. A good AI system explains why it surfaced this issue in very plain, straightforward language. The user can look at the results and understand why the system identified this as an issue. The next thing a good system will do is provide context. For example, when it shows you that someone ordered a boxcar of supplies, it explains that previously the most your company ever ordered was a box of that particular item from the vendor.

In many cases, an issue must be brought to others' attention, so they can deal with it. The workbench should allow you to track responsibility—it knows that you assigned it to Bob, and it notifies Bob that he owns it. The system should also help you track the reasons why something happened, because that information helps you drive future process improvement in a Six-Sigma-style, root-cause analysis.

The case management aspect of the system also helps you efficiently resolve the issue. If you must communicate with an employee or a vendor about a problem, the system can generate an email that is populated with the specifics of this particular incident. It can say the problem concerned this one particular meal or these five meals, and it can name the restaurants where the meals occurred. It can make it a very purposeful and specific email. There is a big difference between an email that says, "You violated travel policy," and one that says, "Here are five instances when you violated this specific part of our travel policy." The latter will have a bigger impact and influence on future behaviors.

And once the email is generated and sent, the system can track responses. You don't need to rely on your memory.

Think about all the aspects of the job you try to do and how you can automate as much as possible. That's a lot more than AI. That's more than analytics.

Keep in mind that not all AI systems are the same. A good system will have extensive features, such as a workbench, and provide clear, detailed reasons for why it finds certain anomalies. But not every system you can buy or build will have those capabilities. When evaluating a system, take time considering the case-management side of the work. How will you respond to the analytics your system delivers? That's where most users will spend their time.

CAUTIONS DURING ROLLOUT

As part of the rollout phase, the system needs the opportunity to learn about your organization. That is accomplished by reviewing lots of historical data. For the system to understand what normal patterns are, it has to look at six or nine months of historic transactions. And during that process, it will find problems from the past.

Many people may think they've got to run those problems down, but there are some challenges to this. First, the system is not as tuned as it will be, and second, that's a pile of work.

When CFOs chase after past problems when adopting the system, they can end up with a team that is overloaded because it's trying to adopt new measures and learn this new robot. (And at least for a period, they are probably still doing things the "old way" in parallel.) It's tempting to go after those old problems, because there could be some real dollars there. However, your staff still hasn't learned the new way, and the AI system hasn't learned as much as it is capable of learning. Everybody gets frustrated and overwhelmed with the process when you try to correct past mistakes while looking ahead for new ones.

Yes, you learn from the past. If you see egregious things, great. But a better approach is to focus on what to do in the next month rather than correcting what happened in the last. You can't improve everything right away. Get a couple of quick, easy wins and continue to tune and refine the new system. You'll become more capable with your robot, and you'll get comfortable abandoning old methods. Build momentum and get better each month. As tempting as it is to chase down the past, it can be a quagmire and can thwart a project launch. You're accustomed to chasing the dollars found in problematic transactions, but what you need to do is refine future behaviors, because that's where real savings are.

If you want to go after that past—fruit that's rotting on a limb, so to speak—hire a third party. You could use a recovery auditor or contract staff. But recognize it's a one-time lump of nonrecurring work. You need a staff, but few organizations have idle hands ready to take on a large project. Everyone is geared toward running things on a steady basis, so if you have a big, one-time project, recognize it and staff for it. Broadly speaking, it's better to focus on improving each month going forward.

5

IMPLEMENTATION: STEP-BY-STEP

CFOs who adopt a robo-auditor should expect their team to be up to speed with the system in about six to nine months. That's when you should do a formal program review. Decide at the outset where you want your team to be by that timeframe. What metrics do you want to report on? How do you want to measure yourself at that six-month mark?

Your primary goal that first six months should be to make steady improvement. Roll the system out in a phased approach. Figure out what your first easy win will be. There is nothing wrong with going after that low-hanging fruit first; as you get better, you can expand on that initial success.

Many successful companies using an AI system in finance perform a preliminary program review at three months. This is best done within the team and doesn't need to be shared with executive leadership. The three-month review is a dry run for what you want to accomplish in six months. Measure results where you've done well, but always look for places to drive continuous improvement.

A common course correction at three months involves how you're interacting with employees or vendors. How are your emails being received? Do you want to refine anything? Are you giving people enough time to respond? Should you copy their boss every time? See what's working and what's not, because there will always be subtleties unique to the culture of your company. The automated system will provide best practices, but they will often be either improved or refined by your company.

The six- to nine-month review is more formal. You want to be able to show the executives who approved the AI system what you've achieved so far and how you will continue to improve going forward.

TEAM TRAINING

A fully immersive, one- or two-week course on how to use the new system doesn't lead to good retention. People go numb drinking from a fire hose that way. We've found it to be more effective to provide smaller bits of training followed by hands-on practice working with the system.

It's also important to start in a reliable, high-impact area. Learn to perform the basics. Then we come back a week later for a couple more hours of training to implement the next capability. You can also employ online, self-paced training to do this. Employees who put the training to work right away cement the knowledge.

The first lesson focuses on the basics of finding a problem and assigning the resolution to someone. These are black-and-white cases that are easily figured out.

The second lesson tackles issues that fall into more of a gray area. Context comes into play at this point; you need to see not only what the analytics produce, but why the robo-auditor produced them. At this point, you reach out to someone else in the organization and say, "Hey, I see this issue. Can you explain it?" Once you have figured out if the more complicated thing is good or bad, finish it through the resolution process.

Go after highly reliable things so you can show results across the organization and show them early. It ties in nicely with the crawl-walk-run philosophy for using the system. Don't try to do the hardest things first.

EFFICIENCY EXPECTATIONS FROM AI

The combination of artificial intelligence and automation dramatically reduces the time needed for the audit process. It should be at least twice as fast as traditional auditing, and more thorough. The system is so fast and accurate that many companies find that they can (and should) stop doing other things.

For instance, you may no longer need to have auditors review expense reports. It's common for the accounting department to examine a random sample of 20 percent of the company's expense reports to make sure everything is okay and that rules are followed. But the number of expense reports that have problems is very low—often less than five out of a hundred—so the vast majority of the time spent looking at the random sample is a waste of time and a waste of the company's resources. A secondary issue is the inherent confirmation bias; because most of the reports you look at are correct, it's hard to discipline your brain to find problems.

With the robo-auditor, you don't need to spot check anymore because the robot looks at everything. It finds only those expense reports that are different or have an anomaly. These reports—typically 3 to 5 percent of the total—don't always have a problem, but they are all interesting or different in some way. Your auditors only look at 3 to 5 percent of the expense reports instead of 20 percent.

We're talking here about expense reports, but this process works for other categories—accounts payable, accounts receivable, whatever.

With oversight like this, many organizations eliminate manager approval of expense reports. The idea is shocking at first—managers must review those expense reports!—but in practice, this saves time and removes an ineffective step. Most companies use automated expense report systems that make it easy for the manager to hit the approve button. With mobile apps, the approve button is even more prominent on the screen. A manager may be diligent, but reviewing expense reports is time-consuming, and most of the reports are fine, so once again there is inherent confirmation bias. Consequently, this review isn't rigorous. And if the manager doesn't review the report right away, it delays reimbursements, and those delays are a source of friction with employees. Why not get rid of it?

Instead, companies using the robo-auditor will get a dossier showing the different types of policy violations it has detected. A manager can take the more effective approach of sitting down with their employees and showing where patterns of wasteful spending affected the travel budget. Managers don't get bogged down in a conversation about individual expenses and why they occurred. Instead, managers have a more substantive conversation with employees about patterns of problems, and that will have a greater influence on future behavior.

INCREASED PRODUCTIVITY WITH AI

In addition to automating the auditing work, an AI system allows you to leverage computers to keep up with great amounts of detail. From a compliance standpoint, for instance, if you don't document what you've done, it didn't happen. Robots can provide a robust audit trail of everything that happened. You automatically have the artifacts you can produce, which gives you a nice win with any compliance domain. Going back to the pharmaceutical company example, even if government regulators discover a violation, your robo-auditor has a record of everything you did. This record allows you to prove your diligence.

By automating not just the analytics but also the resolution process and recording what's happening, the robo-auditor creates a data set with which to improve fundamental business processes. Those can be big or small changes, but by keeping up with the aggregate results of the analysis in a disciplined manner, you can have a real impact. Well-designed systems can enforce this and require that you assign a reason why something happened to put the exceptions in categories. And then you can go back and say, "Wow. I've got a bunch of things in this one particular category. How can we fix that? What can we do to prevent those things from happening?"

In this way, the robo-auditor tracks why problems occurred and aggregates them. This kind of root-cause analysis allows you to redesign and re-engineer things to eliminate the problem. This re-engineering is right out of the Six Sigma playbook of measuring what's happening, analyzing it, and improving the processes. When you manually create and send your emails or call employees, do you track whom you've had to email the most? You may not be doing it in the purposeful fashion that can drive long-term improvement. You don't have a reliable way to record actions.

Most companies prohibit employees from using the corporate credit card for personal expenses. Companies don't want you buying your groceries with their card. One customer found that people often claim they confused their corporate and personal cards, that it was an accident. Once this was identified as a frequent root cause, the company issued new cards with a prominent company logo on the front. They eliminated a frequent cause of corporate card misuse.

Now, when there is a pattern of an employee using their corporate card for personal purchases, the employee can't offer the confused excuse. The company knows it may be that the employee is in financial trouble, and they can offer counseling help. But it might also suggest that they need to keep an eye on that employee, because people who are in dire straits are more likely to commit fraud.

Many things in the business world are in black and white. But some of it is in the gray area, too. You'll never eliminate that gray area—people are too imperfect to allow that—but AI helps you shrink the gray.

An AI system can also save you time by learning the nuances of your accounts receivable. Say your corporate agreement dictates that a customer's payment is due in forty-five days. But one of your long-standing customers never pays before sixty days. The AI system can recognize this pattern of payment in sixty days and save your company the time and expense of sending out reminders after forty-five days. This also saves your dependable customer the aggravation of getting bills they aren't ready to pay yet. And the AI system can alert you when it has been sixty-one days.

6

ACTIONABILITY, ACCOUNTABILITY, & ETHICS

A robo-auditor helps remediate the problems it identifies by showing you the bigger picture. Instead of flagging a series of one-off issues, AI can reveal a larger pattern. These trends allow a company to take action and eliminate the cause of a multitude of one-off problems. AI helps you transition from fireman to fire marshal. Instead of chasing around, putting out a series of individual brushfires like a firefighter, you can step back and see the root cause of all those brushfires the way a fire marshal would. Then you can eliminate that cause and prevent all those little fires.

A good robo-auditing system focuses not just on analytics but also on displaying the results in a way that gives visibility to these larger patterns.

In the financial area, many of the fire marshal opportunities center on the actors involved in the process. It could be a traveling employee, a vendor, a customer, or someone in your accounts receivable department. Many problems in this arena come from people's actions. Frankly, the ERP system very likely works correctly, but many issues result from the actions of people subverting the system, often with the best of intentions. (Go talk to Bob, he will know how to make the transaction go through.) The robo-auditor helps you ensure accountability and ethical behavior by revealing the larger patterns of the actions taken by the actors. These patterns are more important than the one-off issues, and it can be more effective to address problems at this actor level.

BIG-FENCE ISSUES VS. LITTLE-FENCE ISSUES

As CFO, you are already aware of significant risks in corporate finance and have set up your financial systems to prevent them. It's easy for people to notice problems that happen more frequently and design controls to address those risks. But with AI you can pursue things that occur less often, out there on the edges. AI allows you to efficiently and effectively go after the small events or actors causing problems.

In our work across hundreds of companies and billions of expenses, we've observed that about 70 percent of travelers cause no problems. They do what they're supposed to do. If you flip that and look at the high-risk issues, our spend-analysis reports show that about 5 percent or less of travelers cause 90 percent or more of the high-risk problems. High-risk situations are things like extravagantly entertaining a politically exposed person, which puts your company at risk of violating anti-bribery and anti-corruption laws, or billing the company for lavish meals or inordinately expensive flights.

Focus on the People Risk

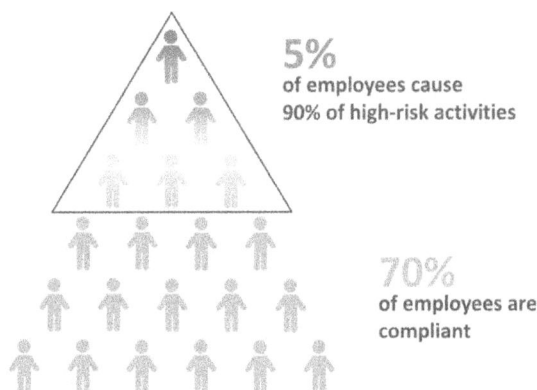

5%
of employees cause
90% of high-risk activities

70%
of employees are
compliant

Not all problems are the same, of course. A friend from business school, Joe Kishkill, introduced me to the concept of big-fence and little-fence issues. Little-fence issues are less severe, such as minor policy violations. If 70 percent of people in your organization cause no problems, and 5 percent cause big problems, that leaves 25 percent who cause little-fence issues.

Big-fence issues are things like fraud that must be addressed with vigor. They are clearly wrong and intolerable. A big-fence issue is when an employee books an international business trip and doesn't take the trip. Instead, he gets a coupon from the airline, sells it, pockets the cash, and stays home for a week. That's fraud, and it's worse than upgrading to a luxury car at the rental car counter during a business trip (a little-fence issue). Both are against policy and a waste of money, but the faked business trip was orchestrated by the type of person you don't want working at your company.

AN EXPENSIVE DOG-SITTER

The Association of Certified Fraud Examiners states that three out of four people who commit fraud in T&E are also engaged in other forms of occupational fraud. Your company needs to distance itself from such people.

In one case, an AI system noticed that every time one employee traveled anywhere on business, there was always a booking at a Spa Paws Hotel. The booking was always at the same location, even though the employee visited different cities on his trips. Next, AI noticed the employee hired the same ride service every time he went on a business trip, even when he had rented a car or used Uber. The ride service was always the same amount. What's more, the merchant category codes obtained from the credit cards did not make sense for the categories he entered in his expense reports.

Further investigation showed that Spa Paws was a high-end dog kennel. This employee put up his dog at Spa Paws and paid a doggy limo to pick the animal up every time the employee left town on a business trip. Obviously, this was not company policy, but he'd done a great job disguising it, tagging the company to the tune of twelve thousand dollars.

The corporate security department took a deeper look and figured out that the same individual had sold over two hundred thousand dollars' worth of company equipment on eBay. He'd ordered inventory, which then disappeared and was found for sale on eBay. What AI found in T&E turned out to be a smoking gun that helped uncover additional fraud.

THE SECRETARY'S CREDIT CARD FRAUD

Another story involves a secretary gaming the system. The first thing AI uncovered was a high number of out-of-pocket expenses. Instead of using the corporate card, she claimed she used a personal credit card. She faked receipts, submitted the expense report, logged it into the system, and, because her boss had shared his login information, she approved the expenses herself.

The first flagged items were that she used her personal credit card in place of her corporate card. When the purchase card department asked about these expenses, she claimed that she'd lost her corporate card but had since found it, so that questionable activity would stop. Fortunately, this whole dialogue was automatically logged as part of the case management process. This recorded history is a chief reason why you want to have this automation throughout your process, because, as the story continues, in six months the same personal credit card issue occurred, and she used the same excuse. When the purchase card team brought the larger pattern to her boss's attention, he figured out she'd used his login to approve her own fictitious expenses. Her fraud amounted to tens of thousands of dollars.

The key here is that without a robo-auditor, these shenanigans don't pop to the surface. The sheer number of employees means fraud like this can go unnoticed. In the case of the guy with the spoiled dog, finding the Spa Paws and doggy limousine receipts was just the tip of the iceberg. The fraudulent sale of equipment on eBay was only discovered after the individual was flagged by the robo-auditor. The case of the secretary shows the importance of having the automation side to help you keep up with how you address the issue over time. The robo-auditor can be used to improve oversight on an ongoing basis.

TAKING AIM AT LITTLE-FENCE ISSUES

Little-fence issues are not necessarily unethical or criminal issues, but they are unreasonable. It's not a case of employees stealing from you but a case of people not operating to the company's standards. Still, they can cost your company money.

AI can help you spot them, too, but the actions you take in addressing little-fence issues are likely to be different. For instance, if you notice a problem with a line item on someone's expense report—say the employee upgraded his rental car or his hotel room—and you go to the employee, the employee is likely to come up with a quick justification. And you can come off as nagging.

But with AI, you can show a pattern of activity and the aggregated impact, and the resulting conversation becomes more impactful. Instead of talking to the employee about one particular instance, you go to them with seven issues that have occurred over the last two months and say that these mistakes have cost the company's travel budget an extra thousand dollars. That's a different conversation. The employee can see the impact, and that more readily influences their behavior. The employee will also understand that their actions are closely watched. The combination of those two messages convinces them to change their behavior.

You also want to consider how heavy-handed you want to be. The first interaction with the employee in question could be an email that doesn't chastise but kindly reminds them of company policy or suggests ways to save the company money. If you need to follow up a second time on the same issue, the system can generate a more strongly worded email and copy their boss. The robo-auditor allows you to spot habitual offenders who may need a stern message. It can also identify those who make fewer mistakes and can be approached with a lighter touch.

An advantage to using AI to spot little-fence issues is that managers and corporate executives can get the heads up that they need to educate employees on corporate policy. How they approach that education is crucial, however, and AI can help guide that. A generic refresher course on company policy will not have the same impact as saying, "Here are five specific places where you violated policy in the last quarter." That message is more direct, personal, and meaningful. It's like going over your mistakes with the teacher, and the teacher explains, "Here is what you did wrong on the test and the section of material you didn't fully understand." People remember that message and change their behavior as a result.

You may notice a pattern of problems in a particular division, or you may find the policy inappropriate for a division and the work they do. Both results can help you improve your processes. If the issues are serious enough, or you've tried the education tactic without visible results, you may need to escalate to their manager, or even farther up the org chart.

When you do escalate, have all facts and data straight so you can have a systematic approach to analyze and track the results. You'll be able to show everything you did and how much cost was incurred, and to determine if the company cares or not. If you escalate and no one cares, it may be time to change policy. Some small problems may not bother you, but seeing them in aggregate may convince you to act on them.

When your robo-auditor system exposes a big-fence problem, you must act quickly and resolutely. However, your reaction to little-fence issues can be more calculated. As you roll out the AI system and get comfortable with it, you can adapt how you react to the little-fence problems. Are you too strident, or should you be more strident? What kind of feedback do you get from your employees? Are you having an impact? Part of ramping up your skills with the system is learning the best ways to remediate the problems that you spot and what type of course corrections will have the best long-term impact.

The fact that 25 percent of your company causes little-fence issues is not as alarming as it sounds. Some of those employees caused only one problem. To get the biggest bang for your buck, focus on those things that influence people with the most offenses. You'll reduce the impact by addressing the biggest offenders. Word spreads, and even the minor offenders will mend their ways.

Your people may not have the bandwidth to run down every lead, so the combination of analytics and automation should help prioritize your work. To be effective, ask yourself how much time you can schedule to address issues. A well-designed robo-auditing system can help with this. If your schedule only allows you to spend forty hours a month to look at problems, a robo-auditor helps ensure that you spend those hours on the highest-impact items and people. That's part of what the artificial intelligence gives you—assurance that you focus on the highest-risk activities. And the automation makes you more efficient; you can handle more issues per hour.

7

METRICS, BENCHMARKS, & CONTINUOUS IMPROVEMENT

The robo-auditor doesn't just find problems for you. It also helps you gather metrics along the way, so you can see positive movement in operations and the financial impact those improvements bring the company.

Your goal should be to drive ongoing improvements in the process. To accomplish that, gather metrics along the way. Those metrics should be organized and correlated with your activities and findings, so you can readily measure the impact. This will ensure you get the planned ROI. It also allows the finance department to set a good example for the rest of the company, demonstrating how finance approaches a problem and measures the impact of the solution.

There is a lot of data to consider and manage. A well-designed automation angle can help with that data. You want to track the issues you discovered, as well as the actors with whom you interacted.

- Did you try to change their behavior?
- What happened to their behavior afterward?
- When you sent someone a gentle policy reminder, what did you see?
- When you escalated it to their boss, what happened next?
- Did the remedial training class you sent them to change their behavior?

This type information can help you measure your current course, or highlight areas to adjust your responses to be more impactful.

The robo-auditor is invaluable in tracking these metrics. If you do this work manually, auditing 20 percent of the expense reports, you probably email an employee when you find an issue. But do you keep track of how many emails you've sent? Probably not. When we put the robo-auditor in place, many improvements result. Emails become more informative. The robot auditor creates custom messages that discuss the patterns of behavior instead of just the one-off issue. The system tracks whether the employee acknowledged the email. You can produce a graph of the interaction with the employee, followed by their activities and problems you find in future months. You find fewer issues with employees you've followed up with, but getting to that point requires a lot of tracking, and it's complicated and time-consuming to do that manually. However, with the robo-auditor, it can be automated, which means it's more accurate and faster.

A robust robot auditor can give you the actual metrics on how well your education program worked and the benefits you gained. You don't even need to go through the data to create those benchmarks. A well-designed robo-auditing system will do this for you; it knows the report you need and has it available to you. This is the advantage to buying a packaged application as opposed to writing one yourself or paying a consultant to write it for you. We have great analysis designed into the dashboard because we've done this for hundreds of companies, millions of vendor invoices, and billions of expenses. We have developed the approach and methodology but also the capabilities for the system to be more and more automated for you.

This automation allows you to reach the second level and become a fire marshal. The first level was recovering some fraudulent expense or rejecting an expense report.

The second level is when you use the system to improve future processes. Much like in manufacturing, it's wise to do a first-level inspection of your widgets as they're coming out, so you don't ship a faulty one to a customer. But it's even better to ascend to the second level and track where the majority of problems surface and then fix the manufacturing process so you produce fewer malfunctioning widgets.

DEVELOPING REASON CODES

A financial AI system can help you get to the root cause of problems. This is Quality 101. Start putting the issues you're finding into categories. To do this, you use something called reason codes. If you know why you're putting things into categories, why you're tagging with reason codes, it's easier to get everyone engaged with the robot auditor to produce the best results.

Start by defining the metrics that you want measured once the system is deployed. For example, employees often say that they weren't aware that a particular action was a violation of company policy. That's one common reason code. Another common occurrence is that a manager approves a policy violation.

It's critical to make it easy for your people to record this type of data that you want to measure. If you know what data is essential and what you plan to do with the data, it becomes easier to tag things with the correct reason code. This allows the system to aggregate the tags to discover root causes. For example, if you see a plethora of "Employee did not understand travel policy" reason codes, it's clear that you need to do a better job of training employees about the travel policy.

Reason codes let you see how many problems occur, so you can direct your corrective actions to the highest-impact areas. They help you see where your efforts as a fire marshal will best improve processes.

Responses and subsequent behavior are also tracked, so you can see what corrective actions work and what interactions have no impact. You may need to change how you interact. Tracking responses also allows you to quantify the benefits. For example, if you have problems with duplicate payments to a vendor who sends two or three copies of their invoices, you communicate with them, and the system will track whether that conversation corrected the issue. The robot auditor and the artificial intelligence keep up with all those layers of information.

It's important to wait for the right time to decide which reason code to apply. You don't want to assign a reason code to everything the instant it is discovered. Usually, you need to wait till you've interacted with the employees, managers, vendors, or customers and heard their replies. A sophisticated robo-auditor understands that and will ask you to assign a reason code at the appropriate time.

The robot takes as much guesswork as it can out of the process. The automation process keeps all the details straight and prevents the user from getting too bogged down in the minutiae. The result is a system that allows you to see the big picture with a click of a button.

REFINING YOUR REASONS

Another way AI can increase your productivity is by helping you more carefully identify where your problems are.

Once your categories fill up with issues, you do a periodic program review to determine how to address the problems that surface. You may also see that one category in particular is brimming, so you may decide to break that down into smaller, more discrete categories of problems with more nuanced reason codes. By refining your reason codes in this way, you can more effectively diagnose the problem and track the resulting improvements.

Don't let the perfect be the enemy of the good. Start with straightforward, simple stuff and refine how you collect the data as you become more skilled with working with the AI system. Just as you drive continuous improvement in your company processes, you continually improve how you use the robo-auditor. If you bought your robo-auditor from a vendor, you should expect them to continuously improve the robot auditor itself.

Say, for example, that you encounter many instances where managers approve expenses that are outside the policy. When you follow up with managers, you learn that sometimes they approve an out-of-policy expense because the corporate hotel rate wasn't available. On other occasions, they approved a higher expense because they wanted to treat an important client especially well. There may be other reasons, and they may all be good reasons, but they aren't identifiable because all these out-of-policy expenses are placed in the same large category of "manager approved policy violation". The category is so big, you can't figure out the real cause of the extra expense. The solution is to create more discrete categories.

For example, your company policy may be that employees can't stay in hotels that cost more than two hundred dollars a night. That might make sense for Peoria, but it doesn't make sense for the many trips your employees take to New York City. If all those New York trips go into a big, general out-of-policy bucket, you may never get a clear idea of why those out-of-policy expenses occur.

But if those trips go into the more discrete category "room

rate not available at destination", you can see that many of your employees violate the room-rate policy because it's impossible to get a two-hundred-dollar-a-night hotel in New York City. So, you change the policy and change the limit from two hundred dollars a night to "reasonable for the destination city."

This kind of policy change is only practical with an AI system that can analyze a mountain of data and calculate valid hotel-room charges on a city-by-city basis. Managers can reduce friction with employees, because now the employees can stay in reasonable places. At the same time, managers can track employees who abuse these rules and can follow up with them and say, "Look, what you do on your trips is not acceptable." This influences their behavior and helps them make smarter decisions.

Creating several different types of reason codes is useful. Instead of only having a code for manager-approved policy violations, add codes for client entertainment or unavailability of corporate hotel rate. Then see what happens. If you discover that a lot of times the lower rate wasn't available, you need to talk to your hotel suppliers.

What you see in all these examples of increased productivity is that your AI system gives you nuanced judgment at scale. It learns that some of your valued customers won't pay in forty-five days. It learns that employees going to Manhattan will pay four hundred dollars a night for a hotel certain times of the year. It tells you about that one employee who continues to use the company credit card for groceries and might need some personal help. This is nuanced judgment that is dependable.

HOW THE AI SYSTEM LEARNS

An essential characteristic of an AI system is its ability to "learn" from the humans who resolve the problems the auditor flags.

For example, you might find that one department is always in violation of company hotel travel policies because that is the way it has to conduct its business. So, that department gets special dispensation. Another example is that the money spent on a hotel room may be different for the CEO, because the CEO travels with an entourage and puts all of them on his hotel charge. Thus, his hotel charges seem abnormally large. You may have a policy that employees can't put alcohol purchases on their expense report, but there is an exception when employees entertain customers.

All of these exceptions are opportunities for AI to learn. You can let it be implicit machine learning, where the system tracks and understands what humans working with the robot auditor do with the findings, or you can allow humans to guide the machine learning directly.

A fascinating balance occurs between what we call false positives and false negatives. A false positive is something you identified as an issue, but it really wasn't, and a false negative is something missed. If you don't have any false positives, you'll have false negatives and vice versa, because some things we look for are in a gray area. Having the system learn from you lets it improve itself. That's why it's important to have resolution automation tied to the analysis, because you create data for the AI to learn from.

THE IMPORTANCE OF CONTINUOUS IMPROVEMENT

In manufacturing quality improvement, there is an expression: "lower the water to expose the rocks." The idea is that you want to remove "work in process inventory" to expose the places where the manufacturing process could flow more efficiently and smoothly. You start by lowering the water (work in process inventory) a little to identify the biggest obstacles so you can remove them. Then, you lower the water a little more until more rocks are revealed. You don't want to tackle everything at once, because it would be too overwhelming, so you attack the biggest obstacles first. But then the process continues, step by step.

In the robot auditor sense, lowering the water is applying new analytics that let you attack new issues. Address those issues, and you lower the water a bit more. You use metrics to drive process improvements, so you lower the water again. You just keep repeating that process, and you keep improving. No one runs out of opportunities to get better.

No process achieves a state of perfection. Your business world is always changing. Vendors come and go. Employees come and go. People using the system will change, and some will be less willing to learn. Some will forget what they learned. That will always introduce new problems.

Or it will introduce new opportunities. You may learn something working with one customer that suddenly makes sense with other customers, so you roll that process out with others. There's always an opportunity for continuous improvement.

As you gain mastery, spread out and employ these robot auditor concepts to additional business processes. It's rare for an organization to have the capacity to introduce the robot auditor to everything all at once. There's a bigger continuous improvement loop asking, "Where's the next place to apply these robot auditing ideas?" and then repeating the whole cycle with a new process. The bigger cycle helps you to optimize your performance in financial operations and cash flow. You may begin by applying it somewhere straightforward, like T&E, but as you gain experience you can focus it on accounts payable, accounts receivable, inventory management, contract labor, or contingent labor.

CONCLUSION

A robot auditor, with its combination of artificial intelligence analytics and automation, should do two things for you. First, it should let you do your job faster and more accurately. Second, it should give you keener insights into what's going on in your systems and give you better control of those systems. You can control the risk but also make things better for your employees. Done well, the benefits of the robot auditor can go beyond the financial processes. They let you change your mode of operation as a financial organization.

This does not need to be a difficult project. You don't need to spend precious time designing how you want everything to work and thinking about workflow. A strong robot auditor shouldn't work that way. It should be straightforward, and the analytics and automation it puts at your fingertips save time and money.

ADOPTING THE SYSTEM

The sooner you can show positive progress, the better. Your supplier can assist with that. The goal is to identify a single area or a small set of easily identifiable issues that can yield a big win. That early victory will build your team's enthusiasm and create some momentum for changes within the overall organization.

After your big win, gradually add analytics and pursue further improvement opportunities. Focus your time on the most productive areas. As you progress through the issues, you start to see the root causes of problems, and you stop putting out brushfires and start eliminating the causes of your brushfires.

Along the way, feed data on resolutions back into the system, which will refine the results the robot gives you. The key to a successful launch is to begin with the end in mind. Have a clear picture of how you will measure results in six months. You'll find it's easier to have the data you need for that periodic report.

Review your program on a regular basis—not just after three months or six months. Give yourself that feedback loop so you can add any needed corrections or adaptations to your process. You'll see those impacts early. Over time, you may not need to do those reviews as often. But never stop doing them altogether. Just like the robot auditor drives accountability in how processes are executed, you need to have that same accountability for the use of the robot auditor itself.

This is an ongoing, continuous improvement optimization process. We have yet to experience where someone who's fully engaged in using the system runs out of opportunities to improve.

PUTTING THE ROBOT AUDITOR TO WORK

Some companies may think they can employ this service for a finite time, squeeze all the benefit they can from it, and then abandon it. It's a mistake to think that way. As soon as the robot auditor stops looking for issues and anomalies, all those problems return. Also, as developers, we are continually improving our system, giving you ongoing access to better analytics that prevent waste and save you money.

Oversight Systems, Inc. loses very few customers. Our customers stay with us because of our culture of continuous improvement. Our system is continually refined through our work with hundreds of companies, millions of vendor invoices, and billions of expenses—a mountain range of data that continually reveals fresh insights that we share with our customers. There has never been a case of a company wringing all the value out of the system so that it doesn't produce results anymore. That doesn't happen. We make it our goal to continuously improve so you'll never want to leave us.

At Oversight, we treat prospects like customers and customers like prospects. We offer tailored demonstrations, and we recommend the analytics that make sense for your company. Our interface is simple but powerful, offering alerts in plain language that make it easy for you to act on whatever issues are uncovered. You go from randomly auditing a small fraction of your transactions to analyzing all of them—and accomplishing that review in half the time.

If you're interested in learning how this system can work for you, contact us at 770-984-4650 or sign up for a demo through our website at https://info.oversightsystems.com.

ABOUT THE AUTHOR

PATRICK TAYLOR is CEO and co-founder of Oversight Systems which, since 2003, has helped hundreds of companies, including Google and GE, improve financial, accounting, and auditing procedures. He was previously employed at Oracle and Symantec before leaving Silicon Valley to return home to Georgia, where he worked on closed-loop controls and artificial intelligence in the fields of network security and finance. Patrick has a degree in mechanical engineering from Georgia Tech and an MBA from Harvard Business School. For more than a decade he has focused primarily on developing artificial intelligence and automation for corporate financial systems.

www.ingramcontent.com/pod-product-compliance
Lightning Source LLC
Chambersburg PA
CBHW022111210326
41521CB00028B/309